AF226002

STORIES FOR JUDE

Painting a picture with words and photographs of memorable moments in the lives of Mimi, Papa, Pari, and Jude.

Shelley Johnson
Glenn Johnson

Volume 1

CONTENTS

Stories from Mimi

The Gaffney House Gaff

By Mimi

I grew up in the small village of Clinton in Upstate New York. My parents bought our two-story grey house on the corner of College Street and Cleveland place when I was just about a year old. When a family settled down in this little town, more often than not they tended to stay many years in the house they purchased. That's the way it was on our dead-end street. All the kids (and there were lots of them) knew one another, went to school together, played at one another's houses, and sometimes got into mischief together.

One summer day when I was six or so, a group of the neighborhood kids were playing outside – nothing specific, just out exploring and having fun. We wandered over to our friend Kevin Marshall's house and from there decided to explore the large area between Mrs. Gaffney's house and Gaffney's field. We rarely saw Mrs. Gaffney - she lived alone, was quite elderly, and mainly stayed inside her large old house. Of course, there were rumors about her, what she did and how she lived, but as long as she stayed in her house it didn't concern us.

The house itself was large with several tall columns across the front that went the full height of the two-story home. No one I know had ever been inside, but from the outside it looked pretty run-down. The formerly white paint was now a dingy, peeling grey and the grass in the front was overgrown and probably more weeds than actual grass. It was always dark and the kind of house no one would think of approaching on Halloween night. The house faced college street and Mrs. Gaffney also owned the vacant lot next door that was always in need of mowing. It was a big lot with just a trace of an unpaved road that was used to access the large field that sat some ways behind the overgrown lot and Mrs. Gaffney's house.

On this warm summer day, we played in the area directly behind, but not too close to, the Gaffney house. We explored this expanse and an old abandoned building, probably once used for chickens, that sat on the property. It was a long structure, but not too tall. We were able to access the roof from some trees that grew close to the back. We quietly walked along the roof till we had a good vantage point for viewing the back of the house. More often than not it was all quiet, but we wanted to be careful because on one occasion we had managed to see Mrs. Gaffney, her back to us, sitting in an old porch rocker in a grassy area of the backyard. Today it was all clear and we decided to take a closer look at the covered patio coming off the back of the house.

The covered patio was rather large (or so it seemed to a six-year-old) and appeared to not have been used in some time. There were a few pieces of dusty furniture – an old glider, some porch chairs, a timeworn patio table, and so forth. A long-neglected planter wall was full of dirt and dead plants. Dead leaves covered the floor, but even as children we knew this had once been a grand place. As we looked around, one of the older kids had an outstanding idea. It was obvious Mrs. Gaffney never used this area, but the neighborhood kids could put it to good use. It would make a perfect club house. Everyone agreed. We each picked out a spot to call our own. Naturally the older kids got the best spots – the old glider, an almost empty closet, the steps leading to the house, and so on. The younger kids were just excited to be included and found their own corners or spots against the planter wall.

We held the first meeting of our newly formed club before we each went home to get the possessions needed to make our spots our own, as well a few cleaning supplies to tidy up the place. Some kids brought baseball cards or cowboy and Indian figurines. Others brought dolls, books, or other toys to fill the spaces they had picked out. For the next few days, we had great fun meeting, playing, and fixing up our new clubhouse. We spent hours there, only breaking up at dinner time.

Early one evening, several days after forming the club, there was a knock at our front door. My parents opened the door to see "Big John Law" standing there. In our little village we only had one police officer and the children of the town had affectionately named him Big John Law. Big John Law had gotten a call from Mrs. Gaffney. Apparently, some children had been trespassing on her property and had even left toys and games on her back patio. Big John Law wondered if we knew anything about it.

We (and the rest of the neighborhood kids) were instructed to remove our personal items the next day and to stay away from Mrs. Gaffney's house. I can't remember getting into any real trouble over this, but we probably were given a stern lecture, and I'm sure my parents wondered what the heck we were thinking.

Pari and the Dentist

By Mimi

When my kids were little, I tried to be a good mom and make sure they were taken care of in every way. So when Pari was three years old I scheduled an appointment to have their first dental check-up. I thought back to the story my mom always laughed about when telling of one of my early check-ups. I was too young to remember the actual appointment, but my mom liked to remind me about the time the dentist tried to look at my teeth when I was little. Apparently when he put his hand in my mouth I bit down and wouldn't let go, even when he sternly (and painfully) said, "Little girl, you're biting my finger!"

As we waited to be called into the examining room, Pari was calm and relaxed, playing with the few toys in the corner of the waiting room. Eventually we were shown in, and Pari climbed into the chair. All was well so far. But as soon as the dentist came into the room, Pari covered their mouth with both hands. We tried to explain that he just wanted to look, but no amount of coaxing by myself, the dental assistant, or the dentist could convince Pari to relax their hands. You would think that three adults could overpower a three-year-old, but those hands were strong and firmly planted over their mouth. We couldn't budge them. In the end, Pari won and there was no examination that day.

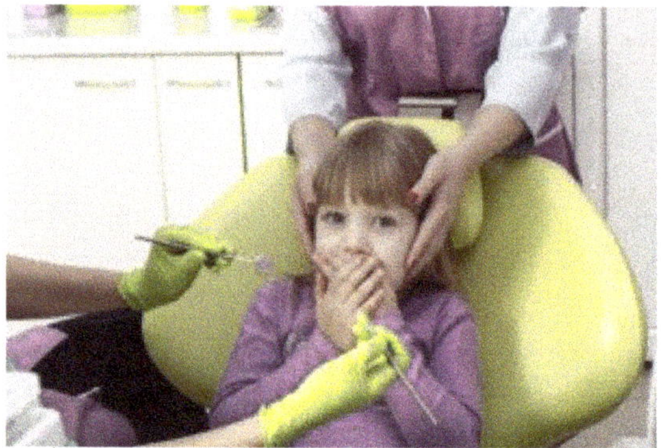

(not Pari, but a good facsimile)

Big Brother and the Desitin

By Mimi

Adam is my first-born child and the one that always gave me the most trouble. He was not quite two when Pari (who rarely gave me any trouble) was born. One morning when Pari was about a year and a half old, I woke up and assumed the kids were still asleep since I hadn't heard a peep out of either one. Ready to get them fed and dressed before going to work, I gasped when I walked into Pari's room. There stood three-year-old Adam with the jar of Desitin in his hand. Next to him was little Pari, covered from head to toe in sticky Desitin paste with their big blue eyes staring at me from a sea of white.

Since Desitin is a protective barrier to heal diaper rash, it is not easily washed away. I believe we had to change the bath water three times that morning to rid Pari of all traces of the Desitin.

The Mystery of the Brownies

By Mimi

One day, when the kids were young, I made a pan of brownies. After taking them out of the oven, I set them on the counter to cool. Needing to run some errands, I left the kids home with Papa. When I returned, I went about cleaning up the kitchen and fixing dinner. After dinner I went to get the brownies, but they were nowhere to be found. I thought maybe I hadn't made them yet, but then I remembered the mess I had cleaned up when I returned home from running my errands. I asked Papa if he had done something with them, but he said he didn't even know I had done any baking.

I called to Adam and Pari to come to the kitchen and asked them if they knew anything about the missing brownies. They both swore up and down that they knew nothing about them. By this time Papa had joined us and very sternly warned them that if they knew what had happened to them, they had better fess up. Still they adamantly denied having any knowledge of their whereabouts. I finally gave up and sent them upstairs to get ready for bed.

The next day as I was cleaning up the kids' rooms, I checked under Adam's bed and guess what I discovered? Yup, a nearly empty pan of brownies. But the most surprising thing was that the kids still both denied having any knowledge of how that pan got there or who had eaten the brownies.

(Adam now claims this was all Pari's doing!)

Adam and the Wax Paper

By Mimi

When Papa and I were first married, we lived in an apartment, but hoped that we could someday own our own home. One morning my mom called all excited. She had seen an advertisement for a small home that we could easily afford. Papa and I went to look at it and it was perfect. It was an older home with just two bedrooms and one bathroom, but it had been completely remodeled. We moved in and enjoyed having our own place. When Adam was born two years later, the house still worked for us. But, when Pari came along, it started to feel a little crowded. After several months, we decided we needed a larger home.

Adam was two years old when we moved from our small starter home to a larger three-bedroom home. Even in a small house, moving is a project that can wear you out, especially when you're also looking after a toddler and a baby. I did what packing I could when the kids napped or when Papa was home to look after them. We had always kept the contents of the kitchen cabinets safe with childproof latches, but in preparing for the move I had taken some items out of the cabinets and placed them on the counter. Of course, with chasing after a two-year-old and taking care of a baby there were lots of distractions. That night before the move I went to bed exhausted, leaving unpacked items on the kitchen counter.

The next morning, I woke up to the sound of Adam running up and down the hall and making a happy, but mischievous noise. Getting out of bed to investigate I found Adam running from the kitchen, down the hall past the laundry room, to his bedroom and back again, all the time joyfully holding a box of wax paper over his head as it's contents trailed behind him. Apparently, he had been at it awhile because the wrap was now several layers thick on the floor and the box nearly empty.

Santa's Helper

By Mimi

Back was I was a child, we didn't get presents or new toys often. Birthdays and Christmas were pretty much it. Even then the gifts were limited. But at Christmas time my brothers and sisters and I each put in our requests for that one special gift and hoped that we would find it under the tree on Christmas morning. The Christmas when was I was eight or nine, I had my heart set on getting a Chatty Cathy doll. There was nothing else that I wanted – just this wonderful doll with the string on the back of her neck. When you pulled the string, she said one of eighteen different phrases. I thought she was the most wonderful doll ever and I had to have her.

That Christmas Eve my siblings and I snuggled into our beds and settled down without a fuss (one of the few days every year that this would happen). At some point I was roused out of my sleep by some commotion going on. I looked at the ceiling above my bed and saw a reindeer leg and hoof dangling through a freshly made hole. Realizing that the reindeer's leg had come through the roof and was now stuck in my bedroom ceiling, I stood up on the bed to see what I could do. Grabbing hold of the leg I pushed it back up through the ceiling. Santa was so appreciative that I helped free his reindeer, that he reached down through the hole and handed me my Chatty Cathy doll right then and there.

I laid back down, pulled the covers up to my chin, and immediately fell asleep. When I woke up in the morning there was no trace of the hole that had been made by the reindeer. There was no Chatty Cathy doll. Slowly I realized that it must have only been a dream. But it had all been so vivid and real.

I was thrilled to find my Chatty Cathy doll under the tree that morning. But to this day, that is still one of the most vivid dreams I have ever had. Sometimes I wonder - was it really a dream, or could it have been Christmas magic?

Pari Loves Disney

By Mimi

Everyone knows that Pari loved Disney World. We visited this park full of fantasy and wonder several times while they were growing up. Pari loved it so much that when they were old enough, they moved to Florida and went to work there.

I remember the first time we took Pari and Adam to Disney World. I believe Pari was five and Adam seven. At the time both Papa and I were working, and the kids were in school, so the obvious time to go was during the summer. It was also my first time to visit the park. Papa had been once when it first opened years before. We were fortunate enough to have the use of my aunt and uncle's condo in Cape Canaveral, about an hour away. This was one of the first real vacations we had taken as a family. Mostly we were used to taking day trips or maybe staying the night somewhere, but this was going to be a two-week trip.

We bought five-day passes and planned it out so that we had at least one day to rest between each visit to the park. Money was always tight back then and this was a real splurge for us. I tried to be thrifty, planning meals as carefully as I could and filling our fanny packs with snacks to eat throughout the day. Feeling prepared, we started our Disney adventure. Everyone was excited for this trip and eagerly anticipating meeting Mickey and Minnie, riding the rides and watching the shows. This seemed like the perfect family vacation.

What I didn't count on was waiting in line in 90 degree heat, an hour or more for each attraction. These days Disney has done a lot to make the wait in line more entertaining, but back then they were mostly just long uninteresting que areas. We spent hour after hour, standing in long lines, leaning against the metal rails, sweating, and listening to Pari say over and over and over, "I'm bored!"

Clippers the Monkey

By Mimi

Most kids love stuffed animals and I was no exception. The first stuffed animal I remember being attached to was "Clippers". Clippers was a monkey with a plastic face. I loved Clippers and carried him with me everywhere. Eventually Clippers plastic face became hard and cracked. It didn't matter to me, I still loved him anyways.

One day I accidently left Clippers home while I visited my grandparents. Grammy and Grampa (my mom's parents) lived about ten miles away. Sometimes, several of my siblings and I would spend the weekend or a few days at their house to give Mom some relief and time alone with the younger kids. Upon returning home a couple of days later, the first thing I did was to go to find Clippers. He was not in my room where I left him. I searched the house, the basement, the garage, even the yard, but Clippers was nowhere to be found.

I sadly told my mother I had looked everywhere, and Clippers was gone. She said, "Oh, that old thing? His face was all cracked and his stuffing was coming out. I threw him away." The trash had already been picked up for the week and there was no retrieving him. It was just an old toy to her, but for me he was my best friend. I was heartbroken.

Christmas Surprises

By Mimi

Christmas has always been a special time for me. As a kid, my brothers and sisters and I would wake up very early Christmas morning, eager to see what Santa had left under the tree for us. But 4 AM was toooo early for my parents. They insisted we go back to bed. By 4:30 we would be up again and gathered at the top of the stairs, ready for our surprises. Finally, at 5 AM, Mom and Dad would get up and go downstairs to make sure Santa had come and to turn on the tree lights. Then we got the ok signal to go down to the living room.

Under the tree were piles and piles of wrapped presents from Mom and Dad. In front of those were unwrapped presents from Santa Claus. There were usually paint sets and a few other small items, plus that one special gift that each of us had asked Santa to bring. Of course, the stocking we had hung on the fireplace mantle were now also filled with goodies.

After playing with our new toys and getting a bite to eat, it was time to open our presents. We took turns unwrapping our gifts, one at a time so that everyone could see what the others got. With eight kids, this took most of the morning!

When I had kids of my own, I hoped that Christmas would be a memorable time for them too. I don't know who was more excited to open presents on Christmas morning, me or the kids. It wasn't my presents that I was eager about, it was watching Papa, Adam, and Pari open their surprises, hoping that they would be happy with each gift they received. Throughout the season, as items were purchased, they would be wrapped and placed under the tree. On Christmas morning presents were passed out one by one, everyone eyeing the recipient as they gleefully opened their package. I loved seeing the excitement on the kid's faces as they unwrapped each gift.

One year as I began to pass out gifts, I noticed that the package was not wrapped very well. Continuing to

pass out presents with sloppily folded paper and poorly taped ends, I silently told myself that I needed to do a better job of wrapping next year. But I also noticed that Adam and Pari were not their usual excited selves when they opened each gift. It finally dawned on me what was going on.

It wasn't that I had done a poor job wrapping. These presents had already been opened and resealed! Demanding an explanation, the kids fessed up that they had previously opened each and every package as carefully as possible and then re-taped them. The anticipation of what they would receive Christmas morning had been too much for them.

This was a stunt worthy of punishment, but I think the kids discovered on their own that it really is more fun to be surprised on Christmas morning. That seemed to be punishment enough.

Chattanooga Choo-Choo

By Mimi

Jude, do you remember the trip to our house when you were 4 years old? You spent several days visiting with Mimi and Papa at our home in Woodstock. We wanted to break up the 8-hour trip back to your home in St. Louis, and although it was less than 2 hours from our house, we decided Chattanooga would be a fun place to spend a day. Just forty-five minutes into the trip we made a

detour to check out a rock garden we had heard was something special. We weren't disappointed. This free display constructed in the backyard of a church was amazing. Scattered throughout the wooded area and connected by nature trails were an assortment of child-size castles made of stone and glass beads that sparkled in the sunshine. Some even had openings so you could stand inside. As we went from one to the next you got more and more excited. The smile on your face grew bigger and bigger as you happily posed for pictures. It was a good start to the day.

We continued on to Chattanooga where Rock City was our first stop. The sun was shining and the spring weather was perfect for a day outside. You were in a great mood as we made our way through narrow stone passages, admired rock gardens and beautiful mountain views. We were afraid you might be scared of the cave, but we made a game of it and you enjoyed every minute. In fairy land

you recited nursery rhyme after nursery rhyme, impressing the group of seniors behind us.

Our next stop was the incline railway. Your excitement about riding in this rail car dwindled when we sat in our seats and you realized how steep it was. I had

to practically hold you down when you started to panic and wanted to get off, despite our reassurances that it wasn't a bit scary. Once we started moving Papa told you "This was as fast as it goes." A relieved smile came across your face as you said, "Oh, okay." Then you wanted to sit in the very front seat to get the best view!

You have always loved trains. I remember on your second birthday we took you to The Transportation Museum which had a train ride encircling the park. Jude, you were so excited it was all you could talk about. With that in mind, we thought it would be a fun surprise to spend a night at the Chattanooga Choo-Choo. As we passed the old train cars on the way into the hotel lobby, you could hardly contain yourself and asked if we could go look at them. We assured you we would do so after we got checked in. The desk clerk presented you with a conductor's cap and wooden train whistle and we went outside to "find our room." The look on your face when we climbed the steps and entered the train car was priceless. Yes, this was our room. "What? This can't be! I can't believe it." You were beyond thrilled.

Once we settled in, we caught the trolley downtown to have dinner. Sitting down next to me, with a heavy sigh, you looked up at me and said, "This is the best day of my life." Mine too, little one.

Gaffney's Field

By Mimi

We may have been banned from Mrs. Gaffney's house, but that didn't stop us from going to Gaffney's field. Gaffney's field was hidden some fair ways behind

the Gaffney house by a thin row of trees. The narrow band of trees encircled the entire field which extended behind the houses across the road from our home, all the way down Cleveland Place, then alongside Oriskany Creek at the end of the road, and around to the back of the houses on the next street over – about a two-block area. It was a big field and its only purpose as far as I could tell was to host a large horse show each year.

Access to the horse show was gained through the entrance situated on the empty lot next to the Gaffney house. Of course, you were required to pay an admission fee if you went through the front gate. The neighborhood children never went through the front gate. It was much quicker and easier to cut through backyards. From our house, all we had to do was cut across the Benson's yard, through Andy Roy's yard next door, then into the narrow, wooded area and through the barb wire fence, already stretched out by our scores of previous visits. This dumped us into the only place in the field we cared about being anyways – the pony rides. Each year my sisters and I, along with our friends, would pick out our favorite ponies and we would ride them as many times as we could, going back and forth to scrounge up more money. If we didn't have the money, we were happy to watch the other kids ride as we petted the ponies that were resting.

We would go back and forth, from home to field and field to home, countless times over horseshow weekends. One year, Andy Roy must have gotten a bit tired of all this traffic through his yard. He was good-natured about it, but at some point we found a black cable in the grass, stretched across our path. Andy warned us the cable was electrified and we would likely be killed instantly if we stepped on it. Giving him a questioning look, I dutifully jumped over the cable. I continued to carefully jump the cable each time I crossed the yard until I finally could stand it no longer. I had to know. Surely, he was fibbing. I stood there looking at the cable, debating. Do I dare? The need to know overtook me and I put the tips of my toes on it. Nothing. I was safe. Smiling I went on my way jingling the change in my pocket and anticipating my next pony ride.

I wonder how many times Andy Roy watched neighborhood children jump over that cable. I wonder how many children continued to jump the cable and how many ended up testing his story. Either way, I'm sure he got a good laugh out of it.

Bye-Bye

By Mimi

I adored my kids and always tried to make certain they knew it. Every time I left the house without the kids, I was sure to say good-bye and give kisses and hugs. Even if I was just running errands saying, "I love you" and "see you later" were important to me.

One day as I prepared to go out, I yelled up the stairs "Good-bye, I'm leaving." Usually this would bring the kids running to give me my hug. Today, nothing. Maybe they didn't hear me. I tried again, a little louder, "Good-bye. I'm going out.", and still no one came to say good-bye. With a heavy sigh, I told myself, "I guess they are growing up and getting too old to care that I'm leaving."

As I started to walk out the door, I heard Pari run down the stairs and yell, "Mom, wait!" My heart lifted and a smile came across my face as I thought, "They do care!" As I turned to get my hug, Pari pleaded, "Will you make me some lunch before you leave?"

The Fight

By Mimi

I was ten or eleven years old when my Mom decided that the family had outgrown the kitchen and dining room of the house we'd moved into ten or so years before. Otherwise, the house worked fine for us. It was set in a convenient location and we enjoyed the friendly neighborhood. Not wanting to move, my Mom designed an addition to our home that included a large modern kitchen and a separate laundry room. The old kitchen became a mud and storage area. The new kitchen opened into the formerly more closed off dining room which was given a facelift - a small old closet was redesigned to be more useful, the floor was upgraded, and my mom picked out contemporary wallpaper that brightened the room and blended it with our fresh up-to-date kitchen.

Growing up with three sisters and four brothers, there are bound to be some fights. Usually the fights were nothing more than yelling and getting mad at each other or refusing to share toys or clothes. But once in a while they escalated. On one such day the family was preparing to go on vacation. I have no idea what my sister Barb and I were fighting about, but it got pretty nasty. I was standing in the dining room next to the wall and Barb was next to the kitchen counter that opened into the dining room. Suddenly Barb's anger heightened as she picked up a knife off the kitchen counter and threw it directly at me. I reacted quickly and was able to dodge it. Unfortunately, the wall with Mom's brand-new wallpaper was not so lucky. I gasped as I saw the knife sticking out of the wall.

Whatever we were arguing about was quickly forgotten as we now focused on a new problem – could we cover this up without Mom seeing it?

Love You More!

By Mimi

Pari always loved their stuffed animals and had plenty of them (although not anywhere close to the number you have, Jude!). I would go in their room and find the animals all neatly lined up against the wall – Pari loved to organize

their things by lining them up in a row. At nighttime Pari would bring them into bed, carefully placing them single file all around them self, starting at their side, up the pillow next to and above their head and back down the other side.

After reading stories and saying good night, they would always tell us "Love you". Each time we responded with "Love You More". Pari loved getting in the last word and with a wink of the eye and a point of the finger, exclaimed "Love You the Most! Gotcha!".

Adam and the Christmas Tree

By Mimi

Christmas was approaching when we moved into our new home. Papa and I love Christmas and love to have the house decorated for the holidays. So, even with the extra work of moving and unpacking, we made getting the house decorated so we could enjoy the holiday a priority.

Pari was just a baby at the time, Adam was two and a half. One day I was upstairs, busy taking care of Pari's needs. Suddenly I realized that the house was very quiet. Suspicion (and maybe a little fear) took hold. It was unusual for Adam to be so silent, and I wondered what he was up to. I called out from Pari's room, "Adam, what are you doing?"

The reply from downstairs came back in a mischievous voice,

"I'm doin' BIGGGG TROUBLE!". I quickly picked up Pari and headed downstairs to find Adam pulling all the lights out of my ceramic Christmas tree. Mischief-maker Adam could always find some trouble to get into!

What the Heck?

By Mimi

Our bedtime ritual was probably the same as most families – get the kids in their pajamas, make sure their teeth are bushed, and brush their hair to get all the tangles out. I sat two-year-old Pari on the bathroom counter and started to comb their hair, large clumps of which began to fall out. What the heck? As I combed more, I realized that Pari's bangs were extremely short. Then I noticed a pair of scissors sitting on the bathroom counter. "Did you cut your hair?" I asked. Pari just shook their head and pointed to Adam. I should have known.

(not Pari, but similar look)

Finger Painting

By Mimi

Pari was a year old when they discovered that they could take their own diaper off. Typically this happened when they awoke in the morning. This usually didn't present a problem, unless they woke up with poop in their diaper. They soon discovered that the poop was soft enough to use for finger painting. We woke up several mornings to find Pari happily standing in their crib, decorating their wall with a new poop masterpiece.

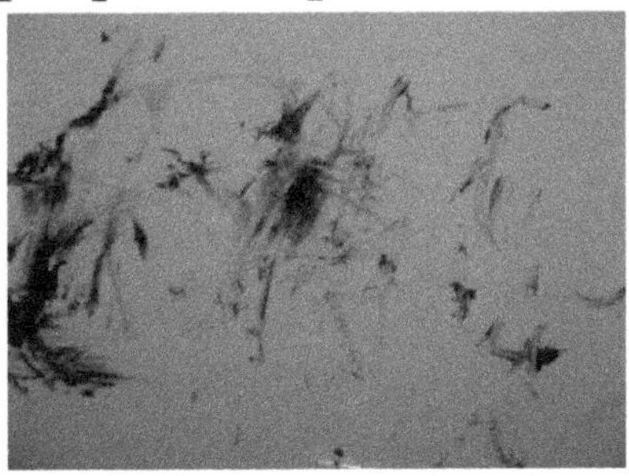

The Space Suit

By Mimi

As a child I was always excited when it was time to pick out my Halloween costume. One of eight kids in my family, I grew up in the 1950's & 60's. We didn't go to the store and buy new costumes every year. Instead when Mom said it was time to decide on a costume, we went to the storage closet and pulled out the large box of costumes that had been used in years past. There were a couple of store-bought outfits like the bunny suit I wore when I was two years old. My mom reminded me every Halloween how I had been afraid of my own shadow when I saw the ears sticking up in the moonlight. There was also the one-piece jumpsuit made out of a thin tiger print material. It came with a tie-on cap and a plastic tiger face. Most of the other costumes were from clothing discarded by my mom or dad or one of the older kids. I remember a white lacy dress we wore with a veil that transformed the wearer into a bride. Then there was a black lace dress that turned whoever chose it into a Spanish dancer. Of course, there were old skirts, scarfs, and bead necklaces for a gypsy outfit. The boys had their costumes also – hobos

were a favorite, and I imagine cowboys and Indians were probably popular too. Each year we argued over who would wear which costume, "You got to be a princess last year." or "I already called that costume." In the end we were all happy with our outfits.

Right from the start, I began making costumes for my own kids. Adam was only 6 months old when I turned him into a pumpkin. Two years later Pari got to wear the same costume (poor Pari was sick on their first Halloween and didn't get to go out). Over the years I made many costumes – a devil, a fairy, a mummy, a cheerleader, animals and so on. Adam liked deciding on and wearing the homemade costumes I came up with. Pari on the other hand liked store-bought costumes. Sometimes they won out and got their ready-made outfit.

One year Adam wanted to be a Martian, so I sewed up a very cute space suit out of shiny green and purple materials. Of course, as had been done in my childhood, I saved all the kids Halloween outfits and stowed them away for possible future use.

A couple of years later when Pari's class was preparing for a school performance the teacher asked if anyone had a spacesuit they could use for a particular number. Remembering Adams's costume from a couple of years prior, Pari's hand shot up and they proudly offered the Martian suit. Pari's enthusiasm quickly faded away when the teacher appointed Pari to wear the outfit on stage. They were to sit on a rocket ship and bop around to the music. Wishing they could take back their offer, Pari reluctantly agree to be part of the performance in front of the whole school. They found their part to be somewhat embarrassing, but I thought they were adorable.

The Dump

By Mimi

Growing up, my family would spend a month at camp every summer. Camp may not be what you're thinking though. In New York State what we called camp meant going to one of the many properties which rented cabins. These properties were situated around one of the three thousand lakes found in the Adirondack mountains. My family rented the same cabin every year at Stiefvater's – cabin number 10, the largest of the cabins and the only one that sat right on the lakefront.

Our days were filled with swimming, boating, fishing and exploring. We spent many evenings at the lean-to across the property from our cabin. Here the families visiting Stiefvater's would come together and gather

around a campfire. As the adults sat and talked, the kids would look for the perfect stick to plop a marshmallow on the end. Then the marshmallows would be held over the fire and be roasted up golden brown and gooey, perfect for an after-dinner treat.

Other than congregating at the campfire there wasn't much to do in the evenings. We spent many evenings grouped around the dining room table playing cards. Our favorite game was Pitch. Pitch is usually played until someone reaches twenty-one points, however one very cold and rainy summer we were playing so much that we decided to start a game of 500 Pitch. It took most of the summer to declare a winner.

A special treat on summer nights was to go to the dump. I know, you're thinking "the dump?", but this was a popular attraction. The town dumped the trash they collected on the side of a small hill, behind which was a forest area. Small piles of trash would be set afire to dispose of the rubbish. Well, there are lots of black bears in the Adirondack mountains and they loved to forage through the garbage in hopes of finding food. This became quite a tourist attraction and campers from all around would watch as the bears came out of the woods. It was fun to observe the bears, until they started to get too close to the crowd gathered around. Some people would start scampering to their cars, but usually someone would snap a picture. Back in those days that meant a large flash going off, which always sent the bears running back into the woods. Show over, time to go home.

Girl's Only Summer Camp

By Mimi

I was not quite ten years old when Mom and Dad signed my older sister Barb and me up for a two week stay at a YWCA summer camp, Camp Alsacan. Our friend down the street, Sherry Boynton, was also going. I was a timid kid and not too confident about being away from home for two weeks. The most I'd ever been away without the rest of the family was a couple of days at my grandparent's house. But Barb and Sherry would be there, so I wouldn't be completely alone. I was relieved that we were all assigned to the same cabin.

Camp was actually fun for the most part. There were lots of activities to choose from and a lake to swim and boat in. We had organized events and scheduled sessions for the programs we had chosen. There was also free time to just hang-out with our friends. One of my favorite times of the day was after lunch when the little store opened up for an hour. It was just a little hut whose wooden windows opened upward, allowing a peek inside at the goodies. Each camper had deposited spending money in an account upon signing up for camp. There were a few souvenir items such as Breyer horses or other camp related items as well as snacks and candy treats.

The worst part of camp was the food. I was a picky eater even at home. I was used to my mom's cooking and expected the same type of food at camp. That was not the case. There were meals and ingredients I was not familiar with and given the choice would not even want to try. I ate very little. One morning I was excited to see that pancakes were being served. Now there was something I loved! What a disappointment to take my first (and last) bite. Rubber. That's the best comparison I can find to the taste and texture of those pancakes. How the other campers managed to eat them, I'll never understand. I went hungry again that morning. Aside from a couple of lunches when they served hot dogs, that actually tasted normal, meal after meal I went hungry. Each day I bought candy and snacks at the shopping hut to quiet my stomach.

The counselors took notice of me not eating and decided that if I wasn't going to eat the healthy meals being prepared, I shouldn't be allowed to purchase sweets. My account was on lock-down. Thankfully, Barb and Sherry came through. They purchased snacks on their account and snuck them to me. I still refused to eat the meals that were so repulsive to me.

The dining hall itself was large enough to accommodate several hundred campers. Each cabin was assigned a table and we sat together for meals. With that many girls in one room it got very noisy. One evening during dinner, someone started, very loudly, banging two pots together. The room became quiet and everyone looked to see what the noise was all about. Standing at the front of the room was the head chef, a short, robust woman wearing a dirty apron and floppy chef's hat. In a very loud and rowdy voice she yelled out "Where's the little girl that won't eat?" The entire camp looked my way as everyone at my table pointed me out. I sank down a little and wanted to disappear.

But no punishment, no humiliation was going to change my ways. I still refused to eat their crappy food.

Paperdolls

By Mimi

Jude, did you know my dad built the bookcase in your room? There is a matching one full of kids' books in our guest room. When I was a kid these bookcases sat in our living room, one on each side of the fireplace. One held our encyclopedias and other miscellaneous books. The other – the one we used for playing – held my mom's condensed Reader's Digest books. Mom got a new book in the mail every month or so. Each contained abbreviated versions of several books.

I hope Mom wasn't trying to keep these books in any order, because my sisters and I pulled all of them out of the bookcase on a regular basis. What we liked about these books were the unique covers on each of them. They came in all different colors and patterns that often resembled wallpaper.

patterns that often resembled wallpaper.

We would pick out our favorites and use them as room dividers as we turned the bookcase into a home for our favorite paper dolls – A Dozen Cousins! This set contained 12 cousins – 6 boys and 6 girls – all dressed in undershirts and underpants with their names embroidered on them. We took turns picking which cousins would be ours that day and spent hours dressing and redressing them and having them interact with one another.

We played with these paper dolls so much that they had to be replaced often. We would ride our bikes uptown to Gorton's, the local five and dime store, and in unison shout to Mr. Gorton, "We want A Dozen Cousins."

Returning home, we would cut out all their clothes and talk about which cousins and which outfits were our favorites. Everyone loved Ida and Babs, while poor Fred and George were our least favorites and always last to be picked.

And sometimes, when we were finished playing, we even put the books neatly back on the shelves!

Thanksgiving Dinner

By Mimi

We had been living in Fairfield, Ohio, a suburb of Cincinnati, for several years. My family and Papa's family lived in Georgia. Some years we would make the trek to Atlanta for Christmas, but most years we were on our own for Thanksgiving. Not being much on cooking, we typically had Thanksgiving dinner at a restaurant, where Pari, Papa and I enjoyed a traditional turkey dinner. Adam was never big on turkey, and all the trimmings that went with it, and ordered his favorite – hamburger and French fries.

They were barely a teenager the year Pari and I decided to cook Thanksgiving dinner at home. We gathered favorite recipes from the family and shopped for all the ingredients we needed for dinner and dessert. Preparation started the day before Thanksgiving and continued all day Thursday. We not only cooked the turkey, but made Papa's favorite stuffing and gravy following his mom's recipe. We peeled and mashed potatoes, cooked corn, rolls and other side dishes. Desserts had been prepared on Wednesday to keep the oven open for the turkey. Pari and I worked together for the better part of two days.

Finally, everything was ready and we sat down to the best Thanksgiving dinner we'd had in years. Everyone agreed it was all delicious. Twenty minutes later our bellies were full and dinner was over. Pari and I just looked at each other. We both knew what the other was thinking and one of us finally said out loud – "This was way too much work for one meal!"

Jingles

By Mimi

After Clippers the monkey was gone, I soon got a new favorite stuffed animal at Christmas time. It was a floppy black poodle dog with a red corduroy coat sewed around it's middle. Because he had a bell sewed inside each ear, I called him Jingles. I loved Jingles as I had Clippers and carried him with me by day and slept with him every night. When we went to camp in the summer, Jingles came along.

Summers, when my family went to camp at Steifvaters, we knew many of the other families that also rented cabins, since the same people came back year after year. But there were always a few groups that were new to us. One of these new families had a teenage boy that was not very nice. As I was playing by the lake with Jingles, the not very nice boy came up and started teasing me. He grabbed Jingles out of my arms and held him up high over his head. Reaching and jumping, I tried to retrieve him, but the boy was too tall. Pleading with him to get my dog back, he just laughed. Then the unthinkable happened. He threw jingles as hard and far as he could, right into the lake.

I cried and screamed. How could he be so mean? I was sure Jingles would drown, but as young as I was, I wasn't allowed to go into the lake by myself. All I could do was watch and cry. Fortunately, one of my older brothers heard my screams and jumped into the lake to save Jingles. My mom hung Jingles on the clothesline to dry and in a day or two I was back to cuddling him to sleep.

The Bike

By Mimi

When you grow up in a big family you get a lot of hand-me-downs. Hand-me-down clothes, hand-me-down toys, and hand-me-down bikes. My first bike was a 16" blue and white bike with training wheels. My older sister, Barb, had also learned to ride on this bike. Once I got steady the training wheels came off and I used this bike through first grade, before passing it on to my younger sister, Joanne. Next, I graduated to the ugliest, faded red, 20" bike with fat tires. I don't know where this one came from, but I'm sure it was well broken in by several children before it came to me. This clunky bike was my transportation throughout 2nd and 3rd grades.

I can still remember the day of my 9th birthday. There wasn't a party planned, no big celebration, I was just expecting a cake and a present or two after dinner. It was a hot summer day and I was playing in the side yard with my sister when my dad came around the garage, acting all mad. He told me to put my bike away. I knew I hadn't left my bike out, I hadn't even ridden it that day. But Dad insisted that it was in the front yard and I needed to put it away now. Here it was my birthday and I was getting yelled at for something I didn't even do. I begrudgingly rounded the corner of the garage and crossed the driveway to look for my faded red bike with the fat tires.

As I approached the house I started to blurt out "That's not my ...", as Dad laughed and said "Happy Birthday Shel." My mouth dropped open and a huge smile came across my face as I looked at my most unexpected birthday present – a beautiful 24" shiny, new, 3-speed English bike.

I loved that bike and rode it all over town – to school, the playground, to the stores "uptown", and to friends' houses. One of my favorite places to spend time in the summer was the community swimming pool. The pool was about a mile and a half from our home, so an easy bike ride for my sisters and our friends. Most kids in town had bikes and on blistering summer days a long row of bicycles could be found lined up by the chain link fence that surrounded the pool.

Late one afternoon after a long day of swimming and frolicking at the pool with Barb and some friends, we all headed to the chain link fence to get our bikes and head home. While everyone else grabbed their bikes, I stood there looking and looking. My shiny blue bike that I'd gotten for my birthday last year was gone. Barb walked along side me with her bike as we made our way home. I wondered if Mom and Dad would be upset with me. Who would have taken it? Was it gone for good? Would I have to start riding the red clunker again?

Dad called the police and reported my bike stolen. It

didn't take "Big John Law" long to find my bike. Whenever there was trouble in town, there was a good chance there was a "Guppy" behind it. That was the name we gave to any of the ten Gillespy children - the wildest, dirtiest, and most undisciplined kids in town.

The bike was returned to me with minor damage, which was easily fixed by our local bike repairman who had a shop in his home's basement. My bike was good as new again and I had transportation once more. My parents bought a bike lock for me, and one for each of my siblings. From that day forward, when going anywhere on my bike, I always carried the lock with me and never failed to use it when leaving my bike unattended.

My Childhood Room

By Mimi

When we moved into the house on Cleveland Place, I was the youngest at a year old. The house had four bedrooms upstairs. Mom and Dad had the largest room, the two oldest boys, Dan and Steve, took the second largest. The boy's room was large enough to accommodate a maple bedroom set that consisted of two double beds, a dresser, and nightstand, plus an old oak desk. I always loved their light brown chenille bedspreads with the cowboy design. My older sister Barb was given the smaller room down the hall. My crib was in the other small bedroom at the top of the stairs. I don't think it was ever exactly a nursery, more of a catch all room used for out of season clothes storage, Halloween costumes, and whatever else couldn't find a home of its own. But, in a way I had my own room for a few months, till the next baby came along seventeen months after my birth. Having my own room was something that wouldn't happen again until I moved into my own apartment at nineteen.

Once my younger sister Joanne arrived, I was moved

into the room with Barb, and Jo inherited the crib/storage room. My new shared room was just big enough to hold a full-size bed, nightstand and a dresser. When I was four, along came the next baby, another girl, Maureen. So now there were four girls. Once Maureen outgrew the crib, the room was cleared out enough to house another full-size bed and 2 girls shared each of the smaller bedrooms. This worked out until baby number seven came along four years after Maureen, finally another boy, Jim.

To accommodate the new addition, the four girls along with the two double beds, were moved to the master bedroom. My parents took the smaller bedroom down the hall and the crib room was once more a crib room, which Jim eventually shared with the youngest child in our family, Greg.

The master bedroom was plenty big for our 2 double beds with bookcase headboards, night stand, and double dresser with mirror - an all matching blond mid-century modern set. Of course, getting 4 girls in one room to settle down at night was not always easy. Besides jumping out of bed to get a favorite stuffed animal or toy, the slightest noise from outside would send us to the windows to see what was going on. Other times it was just talking or laughing, or making too much noise as we played acrobatics in bed. I can remember many a night when my father would warn "If I have to come up here one more time, it's going to be with the belt."

After being in the room a couple of years, Mom decided it needed painting. We were allowed to pick out any color we wanted (we choose a light purple) and most exciting, we got to help do the painting - the novelty of which wore off before we finished the first wall, leaving Dad to finish up on his own. We were also thrilled when we were told we could pick out our new curtains and bedspreads. We carefully selected what we thought was a beautiful purple, green and blue floral print. Then we had to live with our choice for several years. Looking back, I suggest to parents that if you let your kids pick out their own room décor that you reserve veto power.

Getting Gassed

By Mimi

I don't know exactly how old I was the day that Grampa took me and several of my siblings for a ride and stopped by my Dad's office. My best guess would be five or six. It seemed like a typical day, going for a ride in Grampa's car was not unusual. Sometimes we'd go to the New Hartford shopping center and walk around – usually on a Sunday when all the stores were closed. Other times we'd drive out to the country and stop to pet the horses or cows that came to the fence looking for a treat. One of our favorite stops was the zoo. Again, it was typically closed when we got there, but you could drive right up to where the deer were fenced in. We'd go around looking for snatches of grass and leaves to pull, and then would feed the deer through the fences.

Stopping by Dad's office was not typical. We all went inside and found both Mom and Dad there. After Grampa chatted with them for a couple of minutes it was time to leave. As I started to follow Grampa and my brothers and sisters out the door, Dad called out and said "Shelley, why don't you stay here with us." This was an odd request, but I complied without protest, most likely delighted to be singled out for special attention.

Then Mom and I got in the car and Dad drove us downtown to Genesee Street. I recognized the area, it was close to Dr. Obbernessor's dental office, but I wasn't familiar with the building we stopped at. Most all of the buildings in this area were older two or three story structures in varying color brick. Dad pulled into the driveway that ran down a hill alongside the building and we parked in the back. We walked just a little ways up the hill, through the door on the side of the building, and directly into a very small office that had a dental style chair in it. I was put in the chair and a man I had never seen before put a mask over my face. All I could see was black and everything started to swirl around and seemed to get smaller and smaller. As best I remember I was still in the chair when I "woke up."

I later found out that the dentist had removed a couple of my teeth because my small mouth was overcrowded. Apparently, this procedure was done so that incoming teeth would have room to come in straight. Perhaps they should have taken out a couple more teeth, because my teeth still came in crooked.

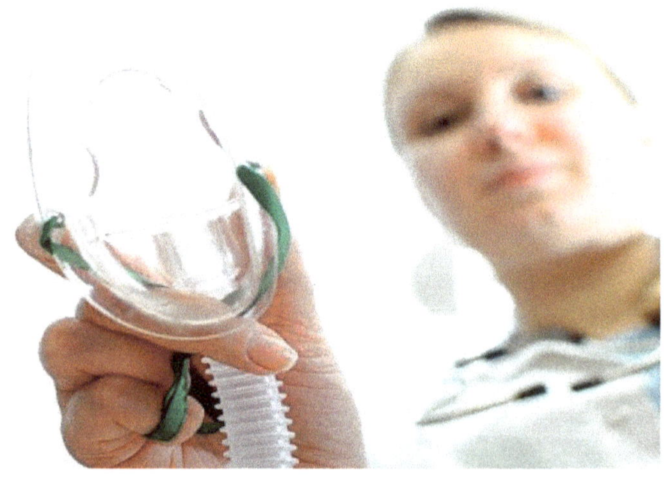

Eating Out

By Mimi

Today it's no special occasion for most youngsters to eat out, but when I was growing up in Clinton it was a big deal, especially if you had a big family. I recall going to Danny's Hideaway a couple of times when I was young. I don't remember much about it except that it was an actual indoor restaurant and we sat at a table with a booth seat that wrapped around the corner. I think we all ordered hamburgers and sodas.

Other than that, the only time we ate out was on the way to camp each year. We'd stop for lunch at The Pied Piper in Old Forge, about ten miles before we reached Steifvater's, our destination. It was just one of those places where you park and walk up to the window to order, and then sit outside and eat at the cement tables and benches. They had the absolute best ever hot dogs and it was always a treat the whole family would look forward to. It wasn't exactly eating out, but we also eagerly anticipated our annual visit to Northern Lights ice creamery, another order at the window type place, but they had great chocolate soft serve ice cream. Northern Lights was located in Inlet, the little town near camp, and Dad would take us out for an ice cream treat once each year during out stay at camp. The only other time we ever got soft serve was when the ice cream truck came around at my grandparents' house, but they didn't have chocolate.

Being Catholic in the 1950's and '60's (don't know if this is still a strict rule) meant we weren't allowed to eat meat on Fridays. Most of our meals were based around some kind of meat, so Mom had to come up with an alternative. We looked forward to the Fridays when Dad would stop by Jean's in Utica and on his way home from work and pick up fish for dinner. To us, take-out food was just as exciting as going to a restaurant. Those Fridays were the only time we ever had fish and I still think it is the best fish I've ever eaten, but then again Captain D's is my current favorite so I guess I'm not a real connoisseur. If Dad was out of town on a Friday evening, it was still a good dinner – popcorn and milk shakes. As we got older, an occasional cheese pizza was also added to our Friday night menu with take-out from Alterio's – no pizza delivery in our area back then.

It was a big deal when Daddy's opened up, in the early 60's, on Seneca Turnpike in neighboring New Hartford. Daddy's was the predecessor to McDonalds in our area and similar to the early McDonalds in many ways – no indoor seating. Apparently it was a popular style back then to just walk up to the window and order. On rare instances, we'd go with Dad to fetch dinner. My siblings and I were all pretty much picky eaters in those days (I still am) and were not exposed to a great variety of foods, so we all ordered our hamburgers plain – just the hamburger and bun, no ketchup, mustard, pickles or onions for us. The hamburgers being small, we could easily eat two apiece. I can still remember my Dad going up to the window and ordering nineteen plain hamburgers – which of course had to be specially cooked. The guy at the window turned around any yelled to the cook "Sit down Charlie, I need nineteen plain ones!"

Stories from Papa

A Christmas to Forget (or Remember)

By Papa

It was Christmas Eve, 1968. We had only lived in our new house for a year and a half. Dad, your Great-Granddaddy, was quite the

disciplinarian and took great pride in the house. He wouldn't allow any of us boys to put posters on our bedroom walls because he didn't want tape residue on or pin holes in the walls. He was also not too keen on us getting too rambunctious, but when there are three boys, we often got maybe a little out of hand.

I was 12 years old that year, Jeffrey was 7 and Eric 5. Since there was a bit of an age difference between my brothers and me, when we played games it was often me against both of them. This Christmas Eve was no exception. We often made up games using the few toys we had around this house. This night it was something like soccer, but the ball was a smaller, hard-rubber one. My brothers were trying to kick it past me through the door into the hallway. And get it past me, they did. One time.

As the ball rolled out into the hallway, I hopped over to stop the ball with my foot so I could kick it back into the bedroom. But something went terribly wrong. Instead of getting my foot in front of the ball, my foot landed right on top of the wall. It was like stepping on a banana peel – my foot shot out before I could gain my balance. I didn't

fall down but when I steadied myself, I couldn't believe what I saw. My heel had gone through the wall leaving this round hole. My brothers' eyes got big and I winced, not in pain, but knowing the scolding and probably paddling that was about to come. Then, down the hall he came, his face as red as a tomato he was so angry.

"What have I told you boys about playing in the house?" he yelled and each of us just stood there, frozen and speechless, afraid of what was about to happen. But that was it – no spanking, no more yelling, it must have been because it was Christmas Eve. I went to bed that night knowing I had really messed up. I decided right then and there that I would not get out of bed Christmas Day. I wouldn't be able to enjoy it, anyway, so why bother?

Christmas Morning came and Mom came in to get me up.

"Breakfast is ready," she called.

"I'm not hungry," was all I could reply.

A little while later, Mom came back to my bedroom.

"Don't you want to come see what Santa brought?" she prodded.

"No. I don't want to come out of my room. I just want this day to be over," I explained.

A few minutes later, Dad came into the room. He was the last person I wanted to see that morning. I was sure he was still angry at me for kicking the hole in the wall.

"I think you need to get up," he said. "Santa fixed the wall!"

"What?" I asked. I couldn't believe my ears.

"Santa fixed the hole in the wall last night. You can't even tell it was there," he explained.

I slowly rolled out of bed, walked out into the hallway, turned right to head toward the living room and stopped outside the door to my brothers' room. The hole was gone. The wall was white. Everything looked perfect. I couldn't believe my eyes. Did I dream about kicking the hole in the wall?

I had a wonderful Christmas. Breakfast tasted better that morning than it ever had before. Santa brought a "grown-up" stereo system with an AM-FM radio and a turntable along with a couple of record albums (ask your Mom what those are). But, what about the wall, I kept wondering to myself.

Mom explained it to me later that evening. Our house didn't have a chimney, so how does Santa get in? Through the front door, of course! As they were turning out the lights getting ready for bed, after all the boys were asleep, Mom found a note on the floor, propped up by a chair, facing toward the front door so Santa would be sure to see it when he came into the house. It read:

"Santa, could you please fix the hole in the wall? It was an accident." and there was a map of the living room and hallway showing exactly where the hole was located. The note was signed "Jeffrey".

"What are we going to do?" Mom asked Dad. "Santa doesn't have time to fix a wall with his schedule."

"I guess there's only one thing TO do," Dad replied. "Looks like I'm fixing a wall tonight." And that's exactly what he did.

So this gruff, no-nonsense kind of guy, that had just had a hole kicked into his hall by me, quietly repaired that hole, making it look like it had never happened, and then the next morning smiled as all of us thought Santa had fixed the hole. It was then that I recognized how much deep-down Dad loved all of us, even through his rough and tough exterior.

Becoming Santa Claus

By Papa

*In 1960, in the Chamblee/*Doraville area of greater Atlanta, there wasn't a whole lot to do outside of spending time with your friends in the neighborhood. There were no malls, there was no fast food places. In fact, there were very few parks as we know them today, mostly just neighborhood playgrounds. But, as a four-year-old, I had come to understand three basic truths (remember – this is in 1960):

1.   *Dads had jobs and went to work every day*

2.   *Moms stayed home to keep the house in order and watch the kids*

3.   *Kids played all day*

On the first Saturday of December, after we had finished lunch (which was usually bologna sandwiches, some potato chips, and iced tea) Mom looked at me and said,

"Let's get ready, we're going to the store!"

I was always up for a trip in the car because it meant going someplace special but was surprised when Mom pulled into Chamblee Plaza (the largest strip shopping center in the area) and parked in front of the Buster Brown Shoe Store. The only time we ever went to the shoe store was to buy shoes and I didn't need any shoes.

When we walked in, I noticed a guy sitting in a chair off to the side. He was dressed in a tacky red fuzzy suit and wore an awful fake beard that completely covered his mouth.

"Go ahead," Mom prodded, "go tell Santa what you want for Christmas."

I walked over and climbed up on this man's lap. I knew immediately that this man was NOT Santa. I could see the elastic strap wrapped around his head holding his beard on and saw wisps of his own brown hair peeking out from under his cheap wig. I glanced at Mom with a look of exasperation and remember thinking "Really, Mom? This guy is definitely not Santa Claus."

"Tell him what you want for Christmas," Mom repeated.

I'm sure I rolled my eyes a bit and recited my list of the things I wanted for Christmas. I don't remember exactly what was on the list but a new bat and ball and a cap gun were probably on there.

Fast forward another year to the first Saturday of December 1961. I was now 5 years old and Jeffery had not been born, yet. Again, Mom suggested we go for a ride and, again, we wound up at the Buster Brown Shoe Store. Once inside, yes you guessed it, Mom told me to go tell Santa what I wanted for Christmas.

I climbed up on this man's lap once again, inspected his face and confirmed his beard was held on by a strap and the white hair on his head was not his own. And then it hit me. I knew for a matter of fact that this man was not THE Santa Claus but I also knew that I told this guy what I wanted Santa to bring me last year and that's what I got so he must have some kind of inside track to Santa, himself. So, obviously, it was his job (see #1 above) to pretend he was Santa to gather wish lists from children and get them to the real Santa. And if this was HIS job, then that's the job I wanted to do some day.

49 years later, in 2010 – a year before you were born, I got the notice. I, too, would get to listen and gather wish lists from children all over and make sure they made their way to the REAL Santa Claus. I got to be Santa's helper but with my white beard as real as it can be and no brown hair peeking out from under my white hair, people wonder "Maybe that's NOT Santa's helper, maybe that IS Santa Claus."

Youth Soccer

By Papa

Mimi and I very much encouraged Adam and Pari to explore activities outside of school, especially to keep them occupied during the summer. Adam tried karate one year and Pari even took ballet. The one sport Adam really enjoyed as a youth was soccer. There were two main levels of youth soccer: Rec and Select. Rec, short for recreational, soccer is usually run by the local city Department of Parks and Recreation or maybe "The Y". This is where most kids start playing, learning the rules and finding out how much they enjoy it and how good they are. All you have to do to play for a Rec team is to sign up and pay your fees to get assigned to a team. The better players can try out for a better team, hoping to be picked to play on a Select team.

Like other children his age, Adam started out on one of the local rec teams. It seemed like they practiced all the time and since I was at the field with Adam, Mimi pretty much insisted I take Pari along to get all of us out of the house and give Mimi some quiet time. While Adam was practicing with the team, Pari and I would pass the time by kicking a soccer ball around off the field. The rec teams were divided by age group. If you were 6 or 7 years old then you played on the team for children under 8 years old (U8). When you turned 8 years old then you had to move to the next division, U10. Pari was around 5 when we started going to Adam's soccer practices.

Pari wound up practicing soccer on the sidelines almost as much as Adam did with his team on the field. After Adam's first year, Mimi and I decided since Pari was at practice anyway, why not let them play on a team, as well. So, when Pari turned 6, we signed them up to play on a U8 team. Pari was not very fond of the idea of playing on a team, to say the least. Pari preferred to stay on the sidelines, kicking the ball around with me and some of the other younger brothers and sisters there. They didn't want the attention of other people watching them play.

This was the first year our local department let girls play organized soccer. There weren't enough girls to have girls' teams, so the girls just played on the boy's teams. That changed the next year when a couple of the parents went to the Parks Department and requested that we be able to form a girls-only team. Pari was a member of that very first all-girls team in Cherokee County Georgia.

The problem was, there were only enough girls to form ONE team, so guess who they played? That's right, they had to play the boys teams! And they lost. Every. Single. Game! But the girls had a great time. They never got discouraged and were so excited when they scored 1 goal, even though the other team had six or seven. The next season, the coach went back to the Parks Department and asked to make the girl's team a Select team instead of a Rec team. This allowed us to travel around Atlanta and play other girls teams and only girls teams.

Something else happened that year we moved to the Select program. The coach, one of the player's mom, announced she would not be able to continue coaching. So, I volunteered and became the first coach of the first girls select team in Cherokee County. I knew we had a good team who played together well and had a good time on the field. My biggest concern, though, was we only practiced on half a field. So I would have the offense start at mid-field and try to score against the defense. If the defense got the ball, they would take it back to mid-field when I would blow my whistle for them to stop so we could play back on our half of the practice field. How would they react to a real game in a strange park, after driving over an hour just to get there? Would our defense get the ball and take it to mid-field and stop? What were they going to do?

We got the ball shortly after kick-off and after a couple of passes scored our first goal. We had our first lead ever in a soccer game as a team! A couple of minutes later we scored another goal, then another. So I called the players over to the sideline and told them that I wanted them to pass the ball at least 3 times to different players on our team before they took a shot. They went out and passed the ball. They did it well! The other team kept getting out of position making it easier for us to score by passing the ball. One, two, three MORE goals. I think it was 6 - 0 at half-time.

Just before half-time, one of the player's Dad came over to talk to me. He was also a coach for a boys select team. He suggested I have the girls intentionally miss the goal when shooting. That just didn't fee right to me asking the girls to miss on purpose so I instructed the girls that in the second half, when we got the ball, I wanted us to bring the ball back toward our goal, that every player on our team had to touch the ball and pass it to another before we could try to score. The girls on the other team were so confused when we got the ball after half-time and started running toward our own goal! They raised their arms and shrugged their shoulders and looked over at their coach. Our team patiently brought the ball back, passed expertly to each other then took the ball forward and scored. Again, and again. 9-0. Then, I just yelled out to the team "Everyone who is on offense is now playing defense and everyone on defense is now playing offense!" I thought maybe our players who were really good at playing defense wouldn't be that good trying to shoot the ball. Ten. Eleven. Twelve. Our first game as a select team and we won 12 – 0!

I asked Pari after the game, "What happened? This team only scored like 3 goals the entire last season and come out today and score 12 in one game." Pari's reply was short and to the point, "It was easy. We were used to playing against the boys but today we were just playing a bunch of girls!"

Sassy-Bird

By Papa

We moved to Fairfield, Ohio, a suburb of Cincinnati, when Pari was in the 4th grade and Adam was in the 6th. I worked on the bottom floor of an office building that wasn't too far from our house. This office building was a little strange in that the first floor was slightly underground, so the bottom of the windows was right at ground level. There were a couple of stray cats in the area and Nancy, one of my co-workers who had a desk right next to the windows, would leave food out for them at the end of every workday.

A couple of months later, it became obvious to us all that one of the cats was very pregnant. Nancy was concerned for the safety and well-being of the cat so instead of leaving the food outside for her, she would open the window and leave the food on the windowsill. As Momma-Cat, as we called her, got more comfortable eating at the window, Nancy would bring the food dish in a little further until one day Momma-Cat was completely inside our office and Nancy shut the window trapping the cat inside. Momma-Cat was not happy but Nancy had set up a cardboard box with a heat lamp and some blankets inside and there was always food and water available. Momma-Cat eventually settled in until she had her kittens, all EIGHT of them.

When the kittens were old enough to leave their momma, we agreed to bring two of them home to live with us. Sassafras, who we called Sassy, and Light-seeker, who we called Seeker, were sisters. It was a lot of fun watching these two kittens play with each other and eventually grow into full grown cats.

At the same time, my boss, Mark, the owner of the company I was working for, had a small parrot at home. I have always loved birds ever since seeing the mynah bird at the garden center when I was a young boy. The biggest problem with having a bird like a parrot as a pet is they want a lot of attention and if they don't get that attention and be quite disruptive and destructive. Mark came into the office and asked if anyone would be willing to take care of their bird while they were on vacation. He explained we could take the cage and everything to our own home and not have to go to his house to care for it. Since I had always wanted a bird, I said I would. I'm not even sure I asked Mimi first. Oops.

Pari immediately fell in love with this bird, a green-cheeked conure, and insisted that she, the bird, stay in their room. We knew the bird would probably be better off with company, especially in a strange environment, so we agreed. One problem though, the parrot's name was Sassy and we already had a cat named Sassy so Pari came up with the perfect solution: we'll just call them Sassy-Cat and Sassy-Bird. And that's exactly what we did. When Mark and his family returned home from vacation, he asked us if we would like to keep Sassy, that she was just too much for them to handle at home. This time I asked Mimi and we agreed Sassy-Bird could stay with us.

You know how good Pari was with dogs, well Pari was good with birds, too. Pari would let Sassy-Bird out of her cage any time they were home and in the room. Sassy-Bird liked to sit on Pari's shoulder when they read or did homework. What we didn't know, however, was that Sassy-Bird was an excellent mimic. There were times when we thought we heard the phone ring and it was really Sassy-Bird but one of the funniest things she would do is in the morning she would sound just like the alarm clock going off then, in Mimi's voice, say "Alix, time to get up!"

When we moved from Cincinnati back to Georgia, we knew Sassy-Bird was not going to be able to make the trip with us. The pet situation was just not such that we could have the bird.

We had a garage sale just before we left to get rid of a few of the last remaining items that we weren't going to bring back to Georgia with us. Toward the very end of the sale, a mother and daughter were walking through the house. Pari had Sassy-Bird with them and the little girl instantly fell in love. With tears in their eyes, Pari asked the Mom and girl if they would like to take Sassy-Bird home with them. The Mom said okay and the girl was so excited, and I know that helped ease Pari's pain of saying good-bye to their favorite pet.

Jude and Santa

By Papa

My beard and hair have been white since before you were born. There are a couple of events that make me smile when I think back on them that specifically involve you and me, as Santa.

The first one was in 2015 when Mimi came to St. Louis. You, Momma, Pari, and Mimi came to visit me in Chicago. Either one morning before the mall opened or one evening after I had gotten back to the hotel from the mall, everyone was in your hotel room. Everyone was talking, Momma, Pari, Mimi, and me about whatever was being planned later that evening. You really wanted to show me something and kept saying, "Papa. Papa. Papa." But I wouldn't turn around to see what you wanted.

Then, you let out a fairly loud, "SANTA!" I got the message right away, turned around and spent the next half-hour or so just with you.

Another year, we all went to Disney World in Orlando, Florida. I like to wear a red shirt when I'm on vacation but I don't go around saying "Ho, ho, ho!" or do anything else outwardly to draw attention to myself. But every so often, somebody in line would ask if they could take their picture with me. We had just gotten in line at Goofy's Barnstormer Roller Coaster when a lady walked up to us and asked if I would step over so she could get a picture with me with her family. When I got back in line with the rest of our group, you asked, "If you're not Santa, why did that woman want to take your picture?"

I explained that some people enjoy seeing "Santa on vacation" and they like telling the kids, "See, you never know where we'll run into Santa", that maybe the kids were acting up a bit, but most likely because it just makes people happy seeing someone who they think is Santa Claus out and about when it's not Christmas.

THEN, a year or two later, you came to visit Mimi and me at our house. While you were here, we went to Six Flags and rode the rides there. You kept wanting to ride the Joker Funhouse Coaster. We all rode it together, then you rode it with me a couple of times, then you wanted to keep riding it so you rode it with Mimi a couple of times. When you got off the ride, you were way high up on a platform. You would look over the edge trying to find me down on the pathway and when you found me would yell down, "Hey, Santa!"

Later, we stood in a long line to get on a ride, I don't remember which one. The line wound around and down until we got close to where we got on. It was also where the riders got off so there was constantly a pretty big crowd leaving the ride as we were walking by. Then, one time, as the sidewalk was full of guests that had just gotten off the ride was walking by us, you stood up on the bottom rung on the railing and shouted out so everyone could hear, "Hey, everyone. It's Santa!" and pointed at me. You thought that was SOOOO funny.

Growing up on a Dead-End Street

By Papa

When I was a little, we lived at the end of a dead-end street. There were only 14 houses total, 7 on each side, and most of them had children around my age. Including me, there were 21 kids on our short little street. We would play kick-ball in the Munford's front yard and whiffle ball in my front yard, and dodge ball out in the street. What we enjoyed doing the most was riding our bikes! Our street was special to us because the water company had come in and run a new sewer pipe down the middle of our street with new branches going off to each house. Of course, when they repaired the road, they just patched over where they had dug to lay the new pipes and didn't bother repaving the entire road. This meant we had our own little highway system right on our little street. We would use the center run as the main street and the branches off to each side as other side roads.

Joey Chitwood had a siren on his bike. It was a little round device bolted to the fender that when you pulled the chain, it would push it against the side of the tire. The tire would then spin the insides of the device and it would make a loud wail, just like a siren. So Joey was always our pretend policeman.

There was an empty field at the end of the road that stretched all the way to the next major road, Buford Highway. To make sure the cars didn't drive into the field, there was a large dirt mound that stretch all the way across the end of the road. Cars couldn't get by but you should have seen us flying over that hill on our bicycles! We would start at the other end of the street by Shallowford Road and pedal as hard as we could and see who could jump their bike the furthest. My bike never jumped very far because I had a big bike with 26" wheels and most of the other kids had the Stingray bikes.

That field was a magical place for us. It wasn't clear by any imagination, but it wasn't wooded, either. It was mostly just overgrown with bushes and a few smaller trees here and there. Summers were the best for two reason. First off, the blackberry bushes – which were everywhere, would have the biggest, juiciest blackberries on them and we would eat them for hours at the time. They were sooo

good. Also, at the end of the trail that wound through the underbrush and emptied out on Buford Highway was the "Fruit Basket" which was just a small convenience store and a Dairy Queen. I remember walking to Dairy Queen on Saturdays trying to decide if I was going to get an Ice Cream cone or a Dilly Bar. They were just a nickel a piece. Yes, FIVE CENTS! Every now and them Mom would give me a dime and I could get my ice cream cone dipped in chocolate. I know you love those.

Pari's Birthday Party

By Papa

We were still living in Woodstock, before our move to Ohio, so it was probably Pari's 8th or 9th birthday. Pari had always wanted a big birthday party for themselves, after going to so many of their friends' parties, so we allowed Pari to invite whomever they wanted. Between friends from school and all the teammates from the soccer team, there were a LOT of kids at our house that day.

Pari's face lit up each time they opened a present and a gracious "Thank you" was offered to each gift-giver. I'm sure there was lots of cake and ice cream eaten and probably gallons of Kool-Aid and Coca-Cola. I don't remember too many details about the party, itself, but we all remember what happened just as it was winding down.

Most everybody had gathered in the front yard, playing and running as they waited for their parents to come pick them up. They were playing tag, tossing a ball around, and of course, kicking a soccer ball or two. Several girls were playing baseball, taking turns tossing the ball to another who would try to hit it with the bat. I think most of them were used to playing with the plastic whiffle ball and bat but, on this day, they were using a small wooden bat.

I don't know why Pari walked over behind the batter, maybe just walking by, maybe to help their friend hold the bat differently, maybe concentrating on a soccer ball at their feet, but for whatever reason Pari was standing behind their friend when she swung the bat at the ball. And missed the ball. And hit Pari right in the forehead. With the wooden bat!

Pari said it didn't hurt but everyone around them started screaming in horror! The bat had hit just hard enough to make a cut on Pari's forehead, and it started bleeding. But it wasn't just a little blood, oh no, no, no. The blood started pouring down Pari's face and onto their clothes. Mimi rushed into the house to get a wet towel, but the bleeding just kept coming. I think Pari was scared just seeing everyone else's reactions but kept reassuring us that it didn't hurt.

Pari's best friend, Jessica's mom was there and volunteered to stay behind with the other kids while Mimi and I took Pari to the hospital. We returned a couple of hours later, the bleeding stopped, and Pari with a big bandage on their head. It turns out Pari had to get stitches to close the cut. You may not have noticed it before because the doctor at the hospital used to be a plastic surgeon so they were very careful about how they put the stitches in so there wouldn't be a scar right there on the front of Pari's face.

I think the worst part for Pari, though, was the cut on the forehead meant no more soccer for that year! Pari still went to practices and went to the games but couldn't play so there wasn't a chance of Pari wanting to do a head ball and opening the cut again.

Our First Home in Woodstock

By Papa

When Mimi and I got married in 1980, we moved into a 2-bedroom apartment in Roswell. It was really all we could afford at the time and the location worked well since Roswell is between Doraville, where my parents lived, and Crabapple, where Mimi's parents lived. It was also easy for both of us to drive to our jobs. But we knew we didn't want to stay in an apartment any longer than we had to. It was a second-floor unit which meant going up and down stairs any time we wanted (or needed) to go somewhere and it was basically just a pain to bring the groceries in every week or so. We could also hear the other young couple that lived in the unit below us. It seemed like they were always arguing, and we just wanted our own place.

After a couple of years in the apartment, we were able to save enough money to buy our first house. It was a small, completely remodeled 2-bedroom home in Marietta. We learned later that there had been a fire which necessitated the remodel, but everything was perfect for us. Adam was born and Mimi turned the second bedroom into a beautiful nursery for the new baby. The house still met all of our needs for our family of three. But when Pari came along, it became obvious very quickly that this small house was not going to work for our growing family.

After a lot of searching and a couple of disappointments along the way trying to sell our Marietta house, we finally got our 'big' house in Woodstock. This was a cedar contemporary which was all the rage in the 1970's. It was still  the 1980's so the design was still fresh enough to love. This house had a huge kitchen and dining room and had a "Great room" instead of a living room. The ceilings in the great room were over 14 feet high! From there, you could go up a half flight of stairs to the three bedrooms or you could go down a half flight of stairs to the 'bonus room'. This room was the same size as all three bedrooms above it, combined, but there were no walls and only a rough floor. This is also where the laundry room was. From the bonus room, you could take another half flight of stairs down to the two-car garage.

The best part about that house, though, was the land it sat on. It was over a half-acre with lots of trees and it backed up to the flood plain of Little River so there was no possibility that anything would be built behind us. There was just a lush, thick forest of trees that you could walk through to get to the river. But we didn't have to walk to the river to enjoy the yard. The front lawn was big enough to play games on but the real fun happened in the back yard.

The driveway sloped down so the cars could get into

the garage but it continued on down to a smooth transition to the back yard. Adam and Pari loved to ride their Big Wheels down the driveway and CRASH into a pile of leaves I would rake together. The back yard had another surprise. While part of the yard continued sloping down, half the yard actually rose to a nice little hill. On top of that hill were 3 huge boulders, or what we called "the climbing rocks". It was so much fun having this natural formation right in our own back yard that we could walk out to and

play on any time we wanted. I think Adam, and probably Pari, too, turned it into their own secret clubhouse for a while. Mimi also created our own nature trail that meandered all around the back yard, going up the hill and between the climbing rocks, then down the hill to the back of the property line,

then back up toward the driveway by our neighbor's house and connecting again at the front of the hill.

We lived in that house until Adam was in the 6th grade and Pari was in the 4th grade when we moved to Ohio. Sadly, someone later cut down all the trees behind the house and turned it into pasture. Even worse, the animals are now all gone and what was once a beautiful forest is just a spread of overgrown brush that doesn't look very good, at all.

About the Authors

Glenn Johnson's Family

- ❖ Thomas Reuben Johnson (Tom) 01/13/1930 – 11/12/2018
- ❖ Janis Louis Bagwell Johnson 10/10/1935 – 2/2/2014
  - ➢ Glenn Carlton Johnson (Papa) 03/13/1956
    - ▪ Michele Johnson (Shelley or Mimi) 08/25/1954
      - ● Adam Johnson
      - ● Alix Johnson (Pari)
  - ➢ Jeffrey Thomas Johnson (Jeff) 09/12/1961
    - ▪ <u>Leanne ??</u>
      - ● Sean Johnson
    - ▪ Dee Whittaker
      - ● Michael Whittaker
      - ● Matthew Whittaker
  - ➢ Eric Jay Johnson 11/28/1963 – 06/08/2010
    - ▪ Barbara Ellis
      - ● Sean Johnson
      - ● Elizabeth Johnson (Loxxy)

Shelley Johnson's Family

- ❖ Warren Earl Hauck 08/08/1925 – 03/01/2003
- ❖ Mary Elizabeth Barry Hauck (Bib) 05/20/1928 – 11/21/2011
  - ➤ Daniel Charles Hauck (Dan) 06/09/1950
    - ▪ Cathy Brinda
      - ● Dennis Hauck
      - ● Daniel Hauck (Danny)
  - ➤ Steven Barry Hauck (Steve) 11/14/1951
    - ▪ Donna Ward
      - ● Daniel Hauck
      - ● Jessica Hauck Gibson
      - ● Kristen Hauck Bay
  - ➤ Barbara Marie Hauck Ayers (Barb) 06/11/1953
    - ▪ Alan Holcomb
      - ● Gretchen Holcomb
      - ● Sean Holcomb
    - ▪ Jim Ayers
  - ➤ Michele Marie Hauck Johnson (Mimi) 08/25/1954
    - ▪ Glenn Johnson (Papa)
      - ● Adam Johnson
      - ● Alix Johnson (Pari)
  - ➤ Joanne Marie Hauck Gillilan (Jo) 01/26/1956
    - ▪ Patrick Gillilan
      - ● Erin Gillilan Haywood
      - ● Danielle Gillilan
  - ➤ Maureen Elizabeth Hauck (Mo) 08/19/1958
  - ➤ James Warren Hauck (Jim) 11/06/1962
    - ▪ Judy Pressley
  - ➤ Gregory Paul Hauck (Greg) 05/19/1965
    - ▪ Jennifer Webb

Acknowledgments

Jude, you seemed to enjoy Mimi telling you stories from the past so it encouraged her to start putting these stories down on paper so you would always have them. As she was sharing some of her stories with me, she suggested that I write some of my memories to share with you, too. We soon realized that the more stories we came up with and the more we browsed through some of our old pictures, there were many more stories to tell. We have to stop somewhere or this book would never get published so this is where we stopped. Since there are more to come, we have denoted this book as "Volume 1" with, hopefully, at least one more coming in the future.

-Papa

We hope you enjoyed reading this book!

When you think of more stories that you would like for us to tell you, let us know with an email, a letter, or even Marco Polo. We'll try to get it into our next volume.
We love you!
Mimi and Papa